ARCADES OF PHILADELPHIA THE PRESENT:

MANUSCRIPTS OF THE 1992-93 PEW FELLOWSHIPS IN THE ARTS

DISCIPLINARY WINNERS IN POETRY

CONTENTS

DIRECTOR'S FOREWORD

CURATOR'S STATEMENT

NATHALIE ANDERSON
6

STEPHEN BERG
8

BECKY BIRTHA
10

CHRISTOPHER BUCKLEY
12

LISA COFFMAN
14

LINH DINH
16

W.D. EHRHART
18

ESSEX HEMPHILL
20

ALLEN HOEY
22

MARGARET HOLLEY
24

LEONARD KRESS
26

DAVID MOOLTEN
28

BOB PERELMAN
30

SONIA SANCHEZ
32

ELAINE TERRANOVA
34

ACKNOWLEDGMENTS

WITH ARCADES OF PHILADELPHIA THE PRESENT, THE ROSENBACH EXTENDED TO CONTEMPORARY WRITING THE MUSEUM'S DISTINGUISHED HISTORY OF STUDYING MANUSCRIPTS AS A MEANS OF UNDERSTANDING THE CREATIVE process. The idea for the exhibition began with a conversation over dinner with Marian Godfrey, program director for culture at the Pew Charitable Trusts. Marian and I were discussing how computerized word-processing affected the manuscript tradition. I suggested that computers were diminishing it; Marian countered that the tradition thrives, especially in our own community. She challenged me to look at the work of Philadelphia-based poets who recently had been designated disciplinary winners in the Pew Fellowships in the Arts program. I took up her challenge with the enthusiastic assistance of Ella King Torrey, then director of the Pew Fellowships and now president of the San Francisco Art Institute. Our work culminated in an exhibition at the Rosenbach (September 12 - October 30, 1994) and subsequently in this catalog.

The Rosenbach invited Eileen Neff, an art critic closely tied to Philadelphia's visual and literary arts communities and one of the city's leading artists, to serve as guest curator of the exhibition. We gave Eileen a completely free hand in approaching the materials and our exhibition galleries. Her choices proved remarkable.

Eileen devoted an exhibition case to each poet, identified by the poet's signature. The cases included a broad range of manuscript materials, from handwritten notes on the backs of envelopes to annotated typescripts to clean computer print-outs. Eileen transformed the manuscript materials into "found objects," using them as elements in often complex, and sometimes beguilingly simple, installation pieces consisting of the poet's manuscripts atop Eileen's photograph of the poet's workspace. On the walls, Eileen installed fragments from the poets' writings, creating a conversation across the galleries' spaces in gold and silver letters.

As the exhibition made clear, the poets' relationship to the manuscript tradition varies widely. Some preserve the creative process at every stage while others, often aided by computerized word-processing, generate no permanent record of a poem's evolution. While the exhibition demonstrated that the manuscript tradition continues, it also made clear that the tradition is in transition. To continue its exploration of that transition, last fall the

Rosenbach instituted an on-going series of single-vitrine exhibitions of contemporary poetry manuscripts in collaboration with the editors of the *American Poetry Review*.

 Arcades, the first of three exhibitions in the Rosenbach's *40th Anniversary Exhibition Program*, received support from the Rosenbach's members and by special gifts from William M. Hollis, Jr. and Andrea M. Baldeck, M.D., The Dietrich Foundation, Peter and Mari Shaw, Charles B. Grace, Jr., Joseph M. Evancich, the Quaker Chemical Foundation, The Walter J. Miller Trust, the Institute of Museum Services (a federal agency), the Pennsylvania Council on the Arts, and the Philadelphia Cultural Fund. In conjunction with the exhibition, the Academy of American Poets sponsored a reading by the poets in Philadelphia on October 15, 1994. Of course, without the cooperation of the 15 poets, the exhibition could never have occurred, and we thank them for their assistance.

 Just before the exhibition closed, Daniel Dietrich offered additional assistance from The Dietrich Foundation. His vision and support provided the spark that gave life to this catalog. Subsequent, generous gifts from Sylvan Barnet and Helen Drutt English assured publication. We are grateful to these friends of the Rosenbach for allowing us to publish a permanent record of the exhibition.

 Eileen's photograph of a 5th-century Greek vase depicting Erato, muse of love poetry, welcomed visitors to the exhibition. Erato's spirit welcomes you also to this catalog documenting a remarkable—and remarkably beautiful—exhibition.

Stephen K. Urice
Director
February 1995

The gift of The Dietrich Foundation is in memory of Mabel Zahn and Seymour Adelman—both Philadelphians who revered books and believed in poetry.

By inviting me to guest curate an exhibition of contemporary poetry manuscripts, the Rosenbach asked for something new. I welcomed the freedom I was given and considered the project's fixed elements—the Pew poets and the Rosenbach Museum & Library—as collaborators in what would be my first experience as a curator. The exhibition rooms, the former bedroom and bathroom of Philip Rosenbach, were chandeliered, beautifully appointed examples of neo-18th century period design, filled with mahogany display cases; naturally, their influence was compelling. The selection of works to exhibit was framed by the poets' recent group status. Expanding the concept of exhibition materials, I included photographic images of the poets' workspaces as backdrops for a wide range of original manuscript materials. I wanted to illuminate their work in a visual field, to respond to the poetry by addressing an idea of the poet. This inclusive approach was reinforced by the installation of poetry fragments—the collective voice of the poets—speaking from the walls.

It was the human trace I was seeking. So it was a particular pleasure to discover a similar urge, an historic context for this exhibition, in the writings of A.S.W. Rosenbach. In his 1927 *Books and Bidders* he lamented that almost all manuscripts of the day were typewritten.

> There is [a] palpable quality in a great man's handwriting which draws one to it; people who have never heard of the collecting mania, will suddenly react to old letters and documents. They are mad to own them. Some human attraction exists in the written work of other years quite different from the appeal made by printing. This appeal is primarily emotional, rather than intellectual.

Contemporary advances in technology make this argument for the human element even more pressing. Nearly all of the exhibiting poets use the computer in their creative process. Several save it for the last drafts, long after the heart of the poem is written. Others go to it as soon as they feel a poem coming on. One said he couldn't write without it; another said she couldn't write with it. What is certain is that the more writing takes place within a technological frame, the less we know about the evolution of the poem; the more disembodied the poet becomes, the more unlikely our interest in the human element will be met.

During the preparation of the exhibition I was encouraged by the support of the Rosenbach staff, the poets, and my friend, Robert Younger. His contribution to the catalog design is a fitting realization of the enthusiasm he expressed from the start. Stephen Urice's intelligent and kind spirit guided me through this project.

Eileen Neff
Curator

Cheek to Cheek

His attitude is understandable—having had the perfect partnership with Adele he didn't want a partnership with anyone else—he was caught in the dilemma of needing a partner, yet wanting to do it alone. In some ways he achieved that by rehearsing with his male collaborator, Hermes Pan, taking Ginger Rogers' role.

Anyone can wear the fresh face, bat the lashes,
make the goo-goo eyes, playing at first love, calf love,
true love. What's tricky is to get the deep sunk tug,
the wrench infinitesimal, that makes it right,
that makes it clear it's meant, and meant to last, to be.
Then you can walk on air, dance on ceilings, swing your
many partners: then it's love, again. Any school girl
knows that in the right arms the kitchen maid turns queen,

so if the shoe's bloody, you keep it to yourself.
Swept off my feet, again, head over heels, I can
rest a minute from the labor of it: mauled corns,
cramped arches, blistered toes. He's under my skin, again,
so I itch with it, hanker to shake it out, kick
it off, shimmy it away—in tune, again, with
a plunked and twanging heartstring. Flashy steps, fast turns:
always someone—thank God—between me and my desire.

The turned head, the flushed cheek, the blinded eye; the skin
aware and wary beneath the traitor silk, the waist
gripped tight til breath heaves the breasts free; the arched back
dragging the head behind, sweeping the floor with hair;
the weak flesh trembling, breath wrung, red rose bled white, thigh
opening involuntary; each step launching
the next, inexorable: yen, rut, bruising, dismay.
I could dance it by myself, what love's done to me.

I LIVE WITH POEMS A LONG TIME BEFORE I BEGIN TO WRITE THEM DOWN, I BROOD ON THEM, WALK BACK AND FORTH TO SCHOOL WITH THEM, REPEAT THEIR FIRST PHRASES AS A SORT OF MANTRA.

6

Porno Diva Numero Uno
4

no one ever thinks of not believing in "I am" ridiculous to
"believe in oneself" might as well begin our next visit there
dramatically because what about delay your name for the large glass this
time he seemed bored distracted but he was amazing his absolute
sincerity the sincerity of not being watched ever of never caring about
being seen of simply being himself though that notion would have made
art is a visible voice without the presence of a speaker a machine a
screen a needle think of yourself sitting down to read you move your
eyes across the words left to right back again left right back and you
hear many things you don't see a garbage truck footsteps birds a kid
screaming you know where those voices came from you have names for the
sources of the voices so even though you can't see the things emitting
sounds you recognize them but my voice HAND even though it's called HAND
familiar thing it does not sound like a sound a voice coming from
anything or anyone you know so it's a voice without a nameable source
all the voices we know have a source we know human or otherwise lines
from a favorite poet whose anonymous source no one can explain define
properly will give you a hint Je suis maitre de silence or La musique
savante manque a notre desir or Un souffle oeuvre des breches operadiques
dans les cloisons you can hear in those sentences the absence of the
individual the presence of a voice without personal intention or
specific qualities my HAND voice is not composed of words exactly though
obviously it must have a sound it's not abstract either somewhere
between a voice that makes sense and a voice like the wind's
unpredictable wandering especially when it's strong enough to hear
clearly is what I'm saying the single hand source activates if you were
to see it you would not recognize it in that sense god-like though I
call it HAND but it would defeat the pleasure I get from the piece and
its place among us its situation to say more about something which after
all in the way I've explained really doesn't exist not even for me

I ADMIRE THE SQUIRREL'S WILD, EFFICIENT DEMEANOR, AND WHEN I AM WRITING HARD I FEEL I'M IN IT THE WAY THE SQUIRREL IS IN THE WORLD.

Counting My Losses

If I begin with the crocuses
snowdrops, then clusters of yellow
daffodils against the wooden fence
heavy-scented hyacinth and bleeding heart
each in the order that it appears
year after year—

if I begin again and stop
and cry for every open-throated crocus,
how many days
weeks			seasons			years
before I'd reach the hollyhocks—
the last of all I planted there?

If I could reach the hollyhocks
I would be halfway through
one summer
but I gave ten years of my life to this
and how many summers
until I recover?

Perennial.
I thought that meant predictable
dependable, lasting
what you can come to count on
year after year anew,
what you've planted being returned to you.

In this garden I grew flowers
and what never flowered:
the lilac sapling a yard high,
a gift from my mother I had to leave behind
and wisteria I started
earliest of all

knowing how long it would take to spill
those first loose falls of lavander.
Counting my losses,
is this where I begin?
Or end—
three more years to first flowering—
I couldn't stay.

LIKE TO SIT AND WRITE IN MY BEDROOM WINDOW—IT FACES SOUTH AND FLOODS THE ROOM WITH LIGHT. BUT REALLY, I WRITE POEMS WHEREVER I HAPPEN TO BE. I'M AS LIKELY TO FIND THEM ON SCRAPS OF PAPER IN LAST YEAR'S COAT POCKET AS IN MY NOTEBOOK.

Alisos Canyon Contract

A child in the affluence
of space and leaves,
I walked out agreeing
with the trees. At my command,
the grand inheritance of the sky,
an affidavit summoned
above the sandstone and
perpetual oaks, a blank page
in back of the coastal range
on which clouds scribbled
my three initials—
proof of everything
left to me under the sun.

I hiked or rode a bike there
for the day-long business
of climbing house-size rocks,
monitoring the white
surf-curls and backwash
of indigent clouds.
       Cars slid by
down the distant road, so many
fish shining through their deep
and watery gates. My ambition
was to gather waist-high foxtails
with my open hand. My distractions
were tangerines burning
like day-time stars in the tops
of the one foothill grove,
a buzzard tilting in his dark patrol.
No one knew me as I
knew myself in my green
and adaptable heart.
Cochise, Robin Hood, Johnny Ringo,
The Cisco Kid, I lived
those lives at once,
and no one quicker
to draw against shadows
or track the venomless lizards
to their hide-outs in stone,
to send a silver-tipped arrow
into the soft belly of a log.
Who knew better the cutoffs
and switchback paths, the crossing
rocks in pools, the free-fall stanzas
of the creek high into the hills
and all the lost Himalayas?

I believed as I was told—
anyone who wished could
have it all. The evidence
was plain as daylight
as far as I could see—
there was plenty, and plenty to share,
would always be—this was easy
as the air.
       And as if that too
were a place you could go,
just by saying so, I stood still
in the wind and claimed
the franchise of the light
across the breathing fields.

Where did I go once
sycamores set their last star-
yellow leaves against autumn
and gave way to the grey
murmur of the boughs?

Sunset, and the yucca
and agapanthus blooms
are at a loss to say.
Here, a dull dusk covers
the days' remains, copperish
as the edge of a coin. Riffraff
of the lesser skies, sparrows
and mockers, offer up a run-down
of my immediate life and times,
the scratch in the dust
I've made, the here and now
beyond the softened margins,
the sea-colored needles
of tamarisk and pine—
the incessant breeze that just picks
at the surface of things.

       * * *

And if I look, as it has become
my weakness to look, for something
to correspond, to pull in to myself—
lure and sparkling spinner—
it's one star shooting lengthwise,
a nylon line cast past the surf,
a flare across the smudge pot night
that goes under with the dead
weight of hope . . . . And memory
sputtering against a screen,
the early outline of that dark
for an instant or so, silvered
into smoke—spokes to a wheel
of vaporous gauze.
       Sky with all
the house lights left on,
floating basin of the Milky Way
shifting left, footloose
in its freight, and no place
now for pity, reflexive as palm leaves
sprung into the windy night.
       This
is the little prayer that wakes me,
calls me back from a landscape
where trees are not cold
enough to be quiet,
has me up early with the wind,
repeating everything ….

I want to tell myself
this is how the world can be—
sky with its citrus glaze, salt
off the spindrift stars,
an aquifer of light.
This is all there has to be
besides the old street to the sea,
where I pray for the gale off the bay,
the belled catalpa leaves
asking, Do you still want to fly?
And the green knowledge
of those sail-shaped leaves lifted
a moment and hovering
like the frigate bird
down the sky to Ecuador.
Evening pulling off its long gloves,
a parchment-white sheen
thrown open above the cliffs
where the blue life of air is forfeit
again to the poverty of my arms.

WORKING REGULARLY, THE POETIC MUSCLES ARE LIMBER AND MORE FLUENT, AND I SAVE A TREE.

Brother Ass

I.
Socrates, unfettered for a few, last, hours,
rubbed his legs and spoke of the body's ills
which his kind must ignore:
he meant the five senses. Do you know

how the soul's fetters are said to look?
Two eyes, two thumbs, shocks of hair
below and above, and it walks
with the gait that your mama gave you.

II.
Its crimes as follows: wasting,
dying. Rotting. Stinking also in life,
possessing pits, possessing mucus. Lusting.
Rooting in stinks: lumbering after
the reeking ovens of other bodies
dragging the undefended spirit
to all manner of high school parties and back rooms
where squint-eyed women line up pool shots
and call each other bitch. And there teeters the body,
grinning, beer foam on its teeth:
it will not be the one sent to hell fire to burn.

But how will we tame it? Shall we make it kneel?
Make it celibate, starve it, as the dancer wastes and hardens hers?
Whip it through long marches like the flagellants
who thought to stop the plague?

III.
Or is it the body that is first of all wise? My arthritic aunt
is visited all afternoon in her fan-stirred living room
by neighbors wanting advice
for she took over what her failing body knew.

The body does not fear: that is the chattering soul's.
The body knows hurt: it pulls its hand from the flame.
It covers its backside with a blanket in the cold wind.
It would not charge the bayonetted enemy line.
It neither rules nor follows, nor cares to teach:
it is merely the bear and the paw at the crack of honey.

A FAVORITE TEACHER, LOOKING THROUGH FIRST NOTES FOR ONE OF MY POEMS, SAID ONCE WITH SOME CONCERN "DO YOU REALLY WRITE THIS WAY?" "DON'T YOU?" I SAID NERVOUSLY.

I refuse to be lambasted by your bloated I Ching

The union goons in their plaid shirts are pouring tar down
every orifice not yet plugged up already from their previous
campaign the 20 years drought better known as the cork stops
here as it does everywhere else for example in all the restaurants
I've ever had the gumption to walk in not to eat but to be
constipated.
I am a man celebrated in recondite circles for his exquisite
stoppages the lips of which have prematurely grown fat from
too much exercise why shouldn't one be allowed an occasional
stump after decades of hemorrhaging wildly at the drop of a
bucket.
Three buckets I have one on each hand and one strapped to the
back of my shoulders the exclusive content of which is the
ossified stools of my past the weight is preventing me from
growing voluptuous like everybody else adorned around the neck
with fantastic ulcers the growth of which is considered to be
highly decorative in this part of the country.
I refuse to be lambasted by your bloated I Ching that ghastly
cross-word puzzle appearing at the back of the Times besmeared
by gum pats darkened through the centuries.
Nor do I care to place in my mouth a piece of rubber band spat
out pre-Christian era from the fatal palate of Genghis Khan
although I am quite obviously one of his more illustrious
descendants.
The physical properties of the world address themselves to me
only in so far as your two pieces of pork fat dangling from
the revolutionary gallow about to be erected tomorrow in the
public square the gala for which I have two reservations.
The noose of my tie is choking me soon I'll be a decapitated
mind permanently hovering over a bucket of piss the stench of
which is making me drowsy.

(CAN ONE POSSIBLY WRITE A POEM WITH A FELT-TIPPED PEN?)

LINH DINH

A Small Romance

Suddenly, to your surprise,
I plucked two sapphires from your eyes
and held them to the fading light
like two blue burning stars. Night

was hard upon us, and the snow
fell in sheets beyond the window,
but we were warm in your small bed
and on your pillow, around your head,

a soft blue light seemed to dance.
I held you tight, a small romance
of sleepy child and sleepy father
singing sapphire songs together

in gentle darkness burning blue
until your breath came deep and you
were sleeping, and to my surprise,
I plucked two sapphires from my eyes.

I ALMOST NEVER USE A TYPEWRITER ANY MORE FOR ANYTHING EXCEPT POST-CARDS OR ADDRESSING ENVELOPES.

Vital Signs
XXXVI The Faerie Poem

I am not the wand waver I used to be.
I realize this as I realize
the changing shape of my body,
and accept that I must
continue to own it
until there is no more
use for it,
until there is
no more purpose
I can reasonably claim.

I hope that
somewhere in the midst
of my grand queen conflama,
I will learn to let go
gracefully,
that in my gestures
there will be
some larger sign,
a broader lesson
to be applied
to the daily civil wars.

Once upon a time
I was black and fertile,
I was virile, coltish,
straining leashes,
refusing collars.
Once upon a time
balls of energy
exploded from
my fingertips,
rolled out of me
in brilliant flashes
that blinded
even me.

Now I ponder defenses:
how to save my life,
how to avoid CMV, pneumocystis, TB.
How to break my nicotine habit.
With twenty-odd T cells
I am nearly defenseless
and counting. I have to learn
multiplication tables, after all,
and put them to wise use.

I am not the wand waver
you may be quick to recall.
I cannot make another thing
disappear. The illusionist tricks
all fail me now,
they draw on my strength
in ways that endanger me.

My greatest feat of all
will not be levitations
or doves out of my hat.
If I can simply transform myself,
win myself a measure of dignity
from my Earth life, accept grace,
then my flight may be free
of remorse, clear of guilt.
I might soar unencumbered
through my shadows,
and sort my way
to other conclusions.

XXXVII

Despite all appearances
I cannot speak with authenticity
for anyone but myself.
Any other utterance
is just stumbling
through hieroglyphics
and prayers,
my enunciation
terrible, at best,
inpenetrable
otherwise.

In the cluttered afternoons
I rearrange little bits
of my person.
I carefully excavate
those memories
that are most delicate
and for that reason
could still cause
harm and injury.
And I thought
these would be my tasks
when I became an old man,
but I am clearly
not a prophet or a seer.

I am a witness
where very few
would stand and testify.
It wasn't always bravery
or duty that made me
rise and speak.
My reasons were
sometimes selfish
and ego-driven,
the moment
calculated
for my gain,
my expansion,
my relief.

Tell me there is
a new political slogan
in the air
and I will learn it
with bombastic verve.
Show me a new
club dance
and I will learn
that, too,
eagerly surrendering
to a new movement.
Now show me
the signs for love,
the practices,
the vital signs.
I have spent
all these years
trying to live
ways of being
I've seldom seen.

LITERATURE ALLOWS ME TO REPRESENT MY BLACK AND GAY EXPERIENCES INSTEAD OF SUFFERING IN SILENCE AND INVISIBILITY. I WRITE TO AFFIRM THAT I AM.

Island Paradise

Against a darkening sky, the fronds
deepen from green to black. The window
frames and flattens everything that he sees:
jagged leaves, volcanic crags, clouds
suggesting the unseen surf. Each moment,
the breeze stirring the fronds and the clouds,
shifting the relationship between these
and the other elements—the slightly altered
hue and texture—, he sees as separate,
frozen, then light ratchets the day
another notch closer to dark. "The dances
have ended," he writes, choosing this pen, not
one of the brushes soaking across the room;
this frail alphabet, not the language of painting,
with its firm notations of color and shape.
That last cloud, a scrap of light above
the outline of trees: once, days ago, weeks,
almost audibly the colors would blend, waver,
submerging in dark. The page dimming,
he scribbles, "the soft melodies have faded
away." Leaves the log open. Goes to his bed.

IN GENERAL, I REGARD POETRY AS A RHETORICAL COMPLEX FOR STRUCTURING THE RAW IMPULSES WE CALL INSPIRATION.

ALLEN HOEY

Brahms' *Requiem*

Elisabeth Schwarzkopf calls it
"Traurigkeit"—"Ihr habt nun Traurigkeit."
Is that what we have now, at eleven at night
with the lights extinguished
and ghosts of headlamps sliding around the walls?

In this concert hall of one,
what you hear is the rough lumber of limbs
being carved into the inner world of the cello,
the trumpet's gold searing black holes
in the chest, new chambers in the heart

as it labors to get its grip again
and again. In the words of Isaiah,
Psalms, Revelations, the Wisdom of Solomon,
you hear a man orchestrating his immortalities—
Clara Schumann, for whom he burned like a candle,

the dead man he loved, the mother
for whom his grief unleashed everything else
—and orchestrating ours, a helpless rebirthing
of ourselves within each other,
the dead being borne in the living,

this conjunction of dust—body of bone,
muscle, and blood already smelling of earth.
How could I have felt it too hard
to contain the "you" I loved and laughed with
after your flesh became "it," grass, empty rafters?

As you knew only too well,
it is not that grief is so beautiful,
but that only the borrowed voices of joy can bear
to rehearse, andante after andante,
its whole depth. Unexpectedly the notes

rise and spill over as ocean spray,
blown petals, parting of clouds, the returning rain,
silence ringing in the bones of the middle ear
and down that mysterious passageway
connecting them with the throat.

THE MACHINE IS FAST AND EFFICIENT, BUT IN WRITING A POEM THERE IS NO SHORTCUT, NO SUBSTITUTE FOR GROPING AND LISTENING, AND I FIND THE PENCIL MORE PATIENT WITH MY INNER EAR.

Sappho's Apples

Every night the screams come through the wall.
Sometimes a woman, sometimes a man, sometimes
a girl-child, sometimes all three—competing,
answering, challenging. Recitative, chorale, aria:

When will you come, my salvation?
— I am coming.
I wait with burning oil, open the hall.
— I will open the hall to the heavenly feast.

The man is usually drunk. He admits it as often
as the woman accuses. When he stumbles up
two flights and pounds on his own bolted door,
the whole building goes into tremor.

As much as when a double-trailer bounds
over potholes, or the el shimmies into its station
by rowhouses compressed into thin straight
accordion pleats—when the spent bellows gasp

For air, after the last painfully slow waltz
has ended. It is hard to figure just what
the uproar is. Turn-of-the-century plaster and lath,
a brick firewall, part us from inflection and word.

So only if the building facade crumbles
down onto the sidewalk, chipped and eroded
brick upon brick in rubble pile isolated
by contractor sawhorses—will anyone really view

What's going on. Then, for a few days least,
kids on course to vo-tech, addicts in line
at the free methadone clinic, laid-offs
shredding lost lottery picks, and young mothers,

Newborns wombed into snugglies—they might catch
the show. The *dumbshow* deep within the second story.
For us it's all *aside* and *offstage*: neoclassical.
Like those Greeks who couldn't bear the sight

Of their cathartic gore (the goo of Oedipus'
raked-out eyes a-dripping down his cheek),
withstood it only in the strict iambics
of a composed messenger. Iambs, and much earlier,

Dithyrambs, almost the same, worship-songs
to Dionysus, whose name means *confused sound*.
Dionysus from Thrace, god of beer-guzzling
northerners, oat and grain mash indigestible—

They spoon up vomit of sacrificed calves.
Retching penetrates the walls too easily.
Six-pack, case, quarter-keg tapped and pumped.
Local brands: *Schmidts* and *Ortliebs*.

The shawm blares out, but beneath is the moan
Of the ball-voiced mimes, unseen, unknown,
And in deep diapason, the shuddering sound
Of drums, like thunder, beneath the ground.

Shards of a misplaced play by Aeschylus, screams
excavated through archaeologic layers
of sheetrock, plaster, chicken wire, lath: Glyphs:
The man might be toughing the little girl.

It's not his daughter, the woman hollers,
But where was she all evening? Out too,
it seems, out on the avenue drinking.
Slut he says. *Don't you ever let me catch*

You doing that to her again she says.
But others are there, hacking, guffawing,
basso voices and mezzo giggles. Encouragement
all around. *I'll flash my crotch if I want to*

Someone says, challenging or challenged.
Followed by the girl's hiccup sobs.
You do that to her again and I'll kill you.
Which her? Which you? Which that?

He comes. He comes.
The bridegroom comes.
Come forth you daughters of Zion
And rush to the wedding feast.

There is laughter: preening, screeching, more
than a glass-pack gunning down the last moments
of his red light. *Will you come my salvation?*
I wait in darkness. The carpenter will not

Raise the roofbeams high. Every night they cleave:
arteries of crazed plaster, a bludgeoned star
as they slip through. Into my daughter's room, where
she flops from sleep, girding herself into a corner

Like Sappho's apple ripening
on the very tip of a branch,
forgotten by the pickers—
No, not forgotten. Out of reach.

IF THE POEM IS TO ENGAGE THE READER, IT MUST PROCEED IN A GRAND HARMONIC, MILDLY DISSONANT, POLYPHONIC, MELISMATIC, AND ODDLY FORMAL MANNER.

The Night

I'm staring at my wife
In her tight black skirt and auburn hair.
I'm watching myself take her home.
I'm watching myself years ago
In my summer-weight wool and Oxfords
Amble along Chestnut from 19th
Back to Broad. It's a lovely night,
The trees standing soft and filled
With light like paper lanterns.
Lives flare in the windows
Like the Little Match Girl's matches.
The two of them can't help
But glance between the curtains, as if
Shopping for a future, choosing a mirror
and brown flowered wallpaper,
Maybe a sofa bed, maybe even the names
Of children. I walk behind them
Trying to whisper in their ears.
They don't know where they're going,
But I do. They half drag, half stumble upon
Each other in embrace. I tell them
To listen closely to each misstep.
I tell them to look, one by one, the lamps
Are going out. But this is the night.
Desire is safe here. And so is forgetting,

Which is where the future begins.
I breathe the warm air and imagine
The love that's coming: her face so close
He can't see what it looks like, his words
So low she can't hear them, and then
The pounding and squeaking of the flesh.
Somehow, I fend off the happiness.
I watch them lean into each other
Like two hands shielding a small flame.
They think the chill is their own adrenalin.
They think this is the night,
The mystery and the passion.
But it's only darkness, and more darkness
As if the match has burnt down
To the fingers, and is shaken out,
As if someone has kicked dirt
On their embers. I wish they would turn
From those stairs, this unlit room,
That they might walk softly away
Before that blanket gets pulled
Over everything, over their poor
Innocent bodies, before it blinds
And hides them like earth.

MY PROCESS FOR WRITING CAN BE EITHER REGIMENTED AND SELF-IMPOSED, OR CAPRICIOUS AND HAPHAZARD. I WAKE EVERY MORNING AT 5 AM AND WRITE FOR TWO HOURS, EXCEPT ON WEEKENDS, WHEN I WAKE AT 7 OR 8 AM AND PUT IN 4 HOURS BEFORE LUNCH.

DAVID MOOLTEN

Chronic Meanings

for Lee Hickman

The single fact is matter.
Five words can say only.
Black sky at night, reasonably.
I am, the irrational residue.

Blown up chain link fence.
Next morning stronger than ever.
Midnight the pain is almost.
The train seems practically expressive.

A story familiar as a.
Society has broken into bands.
The nineteenth century was sure.
Characters in the withering capital.

The heroic figure straddled the.
The clouds enveloped the tallest.
Tens of thousands of drops.
The monster struggled with Milton.

On our wedding night I.
The sorrow burned deeper than.
Grimly I pursued what violence.
A trap, a catch, a.

Fans stand up, yelling their.
Lights go off in houses.
A fictional look, not quite.
To be able to talk.

The coffee sounds intruiging but.
She put her cards on.
What had been comfortable subjectivity.
The lesson we can each.

Not enough time to thoroughly.
Structure announces structure and takes.
He caught his breath in.
The vista disclosed no immediate.

Alone with a pun in.
The clock face and the.
Rock of ages, a modern.
I think I had better.

Now this particular mall seemed.
The bag of groceries had.
Whether a biographical junkheap or.
In no sense do I.

These fields make me feel.
Mount Rushmore in a sonnet.
Some in the party tried.
So it's not as if.

That always happened until one.
She spread her arms and.
The sky if anything grew.
Which left a lot of.

No one could help it.
I ran farther than I.
That wasn't a good one.
Now put down your pencils.

They won't pull that over.
Standing up to the Empire.
Stop it, screaming in a.
The smell of pine needles.

Economics is not my strong.
Until one of us reads.
I took a breath, then.
The singular heroic vision, unilaterally.

Voices imitate the very words.
Bed was one place where.
A personal life, a toaster.
Memorized experience can't be completely.

The impossibility of the simplest.
So shut the fucking thing.
Now I've gone and put.
But that makes the world.

The point I am trying .
Like a cartoon worm on.
A physical mouth without speech.
If taken to an extreme.

The phone is for someone.
The next second it seemed.
But did that really mean.
Yet Los Angeles is full.

Naturally enough I turn to.
Some things are reversible, some.
You don't have that choice.
I'm going to Jo's for.

Now I've heard everything, he.
One time when I used.
The amount of dissatisfaction involved.
The weather isn't all it's.

You'd think people would have.
Or that they would invent.
At least if the emotional.
The presence of an illusion.

Symbiosis of home and prison.
Then, having become superfluous, time.
One has to give to.
Taste: the first and last.

I remember the look in.
It was the first time.
Some gorgeous swelling feeling that.
Success which owes its fortune.

Come what may it can't.
There are a number of.
But there is only one.
That's why I want to.

I WANT MY POEMS TO BE SITES WHERE RANGES OF WORDS MEET.

elegy
   (for MOVE* and Philadelphia)

1.

philadelphia
   a disguised southern city
squatting in the eastern pass of
colleges cathedrals and cowboys.
philadelphia. a phalanx of parsons
and auctioneers
   modern gladiators
erasing the delirium of death from their shields
while houses burn out of control.

2.

c'mon girl hurry on down to osage st
they're roasting in the fire
smell the dreadlocks and blk/ skins
roasting in the fire.

c'mon newsmen and tvmen
hurryondown to osage st and
when you have chloroformed the city
and after you have stitched up your words
hurry on downtown for sanctuary
in taverns and corporations

and the blood is not yet dry.

3.

how does one scream in thunder?

4.

they are combing the morning for shadows
and screams tongue-tied without faces
look. over there. one eye
escaping from its skin
and our heartbeats slowdown to a drawl
and the kingfisher calls out from his downtown capital
and the pinstriped general reenlists
his tongue for combat
and the police come like twin seasons of drought and flood.
they're combing the city for lifeliberty and
the pursuit of happiness.

5.

how does one city scream in thunder?

6.

hide us O lord
deliver us from our nakedness.
exile us from our laughter
give us this day our rest from seduction
peeling us down to our veins.

and the tower was like no other.   amen.
and the streets escaped under the
cover of darkness   amen.
and the voices called out from
their wounds   amen.
and the fire circumcised the city   amen.

7.

who anointeth this city with napalm?   (i say)
who giveth this city in holy infanticide?

8.

beyond the mornings and afternoons
and deaths detonating the city.
beyond the tourist roadhouses
trading in lobotomies
there is a glimpse of earth
this prodigal earth.
beyond edicts and commandments
commissioned by puritans
there are people
navigating the breath of hurricanes.
beyond concerts and football
and mummers strutting their
sequined processionals.
there is this earth. this country. this city.
this people.
collecting skeletons from waiting rooms
lying in wait. for honor and peace.
one day.

* MOVE: a philadelphia based back to nature group whose head-quarters was bombed by the police on May 13, 1985, killing men, women and children. An entire city block was destroyed by fire.

> I SHARPEN THREE PENCILS, PLACE THEM ONTO THE DESK AND I PUT OUT THREE BOOKS BY MY FAVORITE AUTHORS FOR INSPIRATIONAL READING.

32

The Stand-Up Shtetl

"Not until a shtetl had its own cemetery
was it truly considered a *Kehillah Kedosha*,
a Holy Community in Israel."
  —*The Paper Shtetl : A Complete Model
  of an Eastern European Jewish Town*

Let the wind and rain start with a sigh,
over and over. Then you who have forgotten,
you who never knew, cut out the paper pieces;
score and fold them back. Where the instructions
call for bending or curling, determine
how far to bend, how tightly to curl.

It is nearly Rosh Hashonah. The blacksmith
is forging good luck for all this new year.
Likewise, the feather plucker, with his goose down,
is laying the groundwork for a year's
innocent sleep. "From your mouth to God's ear,"
the townspeople greet one another,
although some will wander, with open collars,
with exposed throats, into the path
of thundering Cossacks. You may ask, Is this
where it leads, all the whispering to God?

Still, it is remarkable, how these characters
can be cut out of the bitter story
whole and looking so well.
These two young girls trading secrets
by a tree, who stare into each other's faces,
are a single piece made with one V fold.

The nearest house is in darkness.
But when the walls of the next are folded back,
they form right angles with a newly swept floor.
Push out the chimney with a pencil and smoke curls.
The woman inside lets the boiling water
hurry her. The Sabbath feast is approaching.
Bend the woman's head forward. Fold her arms
over her eyes, carrying the darkness to them

as she makes her blessing over the candles.
Now the *shames*, who all week ferries
the smaller boys to *chedar*, knocks
on her shutter, bringing the Sabbath.

Horses, goats and chickens feed in the yards.
Each has a right and a left side,
touching back to back, though only one tail.
Curve the horse's neck gently, likewise,
the goat's. Bend the tail down and the legs in,
slightly, for balance and to make them stand.

Move on to the market. Take up this man,
the peddlar. Perhaps he is a buyer
of the clothes of the dead. Bend him
forward at the elbows, allowing him to grip
his pushcart. As you do, watch him look up
from under that forward-jutting cap
which focuses his will and concentration.
Bend one leg forward and the other back.
His is a sad business. Expect him
to appear exhausted by it or discouraged.

Then turn a corner to the synagogue.
It is formed of two connecting pieces.
No cuts or marks should be made
on the unseen, inner side. Curl the rabbi's beard
and tilt it behind the podium. Put a bend
in the Torah reader's back. He should look down
at the words, not insolently up into God's eye.

Leave space at the center for a wedding.
As the bride and groom grind the wineglass
of misfortune underfoot, bend the musician's right arm
around in front until his bow strikes the violin.
Then arrange the men in a semicircle, dancing.
Lift their knees. Fling their arms around
each others' shoulders, so that, kicking and bouncing,
they are open to anything.
Each step in their dance will move the world forward.

Do not forget the dead we keep with us always.
On the right, fold the headstones upright,
those for the chairmaker and the tailor, and for
the water carrier whose father and grandfather

were also water carriers. Group the graves
to form a cemetery. The state may forbid this,
since the dead lay claim to the earth.
But if a cemetery is allowed, stand the trees
on the angle formed at the base. Bring in
a watchman and paid mourners. Bow the trees down
in the wind or extend them like the wings
of enormous birds. Bend the darkest branches
outward to surround it, to cherish it.

IT SEEMS I'M ALWAYS TAKING NOTES, ON TRAINS, IN MUSEUMS, WAKING UP FROM DREAMS.

ELAINE TERRANOVA

ACKNOWLEDGMENTS

NATHALIE ANDERSON "Cheek to Cheek" from the "Following Fred Astaire" series, 1990, by permission of the author.

STEPHEN BERG "Porno Diva Numero Uno" © copyright 1995 by Stephen Berg.

BECKY BIRTHA "Counting My Losses," © copyright 1991 by Becky Birtha, is reprinted from *The Forbidden Poems*, Seal Press, Seattle, by permission of the publisher.

CHRISTOPHER BUCKLEY "Alisos Canyon Contract" is reprinted from *Crazy Horse*, 1993, by permission of the author.

LISA COFFMAN "Brother Ass" is reprinted from *West Branch*, 1990, by permission of the author.

LINH DINH "I Refuse To Be Lambasted By Your Bloated I-Ching" is reprinted from *Sulfur*, 1995, by permission of the author.

W.D. EHRHART "A Small Romance" is reprinted from *Just for Laughs* by W.D. Ehrhart, Vietnam Generation & Burning Cities Press, 1990, by permission of the author.

ESSEX HEMPHILL "Vital Signs" is reprinted from *Life Sentences*, Mercury House, 1994, by permission of the author.

ALLEN HOEY "Island Paradise" © copyright 1995 by Allen Hoey.

MARGARET HOLLEY "Brahms' Requiem" is reprinted from *Morning Star*, Copper Beech Press, 1992, by permission of the author.

LEONARD KRESS "Sappho's Apples" © copyright 1995 by Leonard Kress.

DAVID MOOLTEN "The Night" is reprinted from *Plums & Ashes*, Northeastern University Press, 1994, by permission of the publisher and author.

BOB PERELMAN "Chronic Meanings" is reprinted from *Virtual Reality*, Roof Press, 1993, by permission of the author.

SONIA SANCHEZ "elegy (for MOVE* and Philadelphia)" is reprinted from *Under a Soprano Sky*, Africa World Press, Inc., 1987, by permission of the author.

ELAINE TERRANOVA "The Stand-Up Shtetl" is reprinted from *Songs for Our Voices*, The Judah L. Magnes Museum, 1993, by permission of the author.